MW00775123

STAR Projects
INIQUITY – TRINITY – THE LAW

Scott Stanley

This book is from the first three
STAR Projects that can be found at:
youtube.com/@DTGm
www.dtgrev.org

Copyright © 2023 Scott Stanley.

All Rights Reserved.

ISBN: 978-1-916954-97-7

No Part of this book may be produced, stored in a retrieval system, or transmitted by any means without the written permission of the author.

Dedications

In unwavering dedication, this tribute is offered to those with attentive hearts and open minds – those who seek God's kingdom in spirit and truth.

To all who have ears to hear, you are the torchbearers of knowledge, the ones who heed the whispers of the spirit amidst the noise of the world. Your receptiveness illuminates the path of understanding and fosters a profound connection to the completion of your faith.

May this dedication serve as a beacon, honoring your love of truth and discernment of the deep things of God. Your quest to listen, learn, and grow inspires us all to embrace the healing of God's knowledge, leading us into the day of the latter rain.

About the Author

Scott Stanley loves the truth. His conversion to Christ, in December of 1979, had a profound effect, moving him to give his life searching for the deep things of God.

Scott's aim is to prepare Gods people for what is coming on the earth by giving them the spiritual tools needed to overcome iniquity and sin. Bible truth is life to the hungry soul and Scott's teachings will lead you along the path of the eternal Spirit. He will share the spiritual blessings of the heavenlies in Christ.

Born in Oklahoma, Scott is the founder of DTG ministries located in Michigan. He and his wife Martha have been married 28 years.

Scott Stanley

DTGRev.org

scottstanley@dtgrev.org

Exploring the Deep Things of God

Table of Contents

INIQUITY PART A
INTRODUCTION

Hi. I'm Scott Stanley. I am the founder of DTG Ministries. DTG is an acronym for the Deep Things of God. For the longest time, I have wanted to create a podcast and just do a series of studies, making them short but connecting them together to try to bring the gospel to the world, and I just held back from calling it a podcast. I finally realized why that is. In the scriptures, the word "angel" is simply the word "messenger." That word was transliterated and if you translate "angel," it just means "a messenger." In *Revelation 1*, Christ tells us that *the candlesticks are the churches, but the stars, the seven stars that He holds in His right hand, are messengers, or angels to the churches.* I thought, well, wouldn't that be great? Instead of giving messages to the churches, which is what I've been doing most of my Christian life, I would like to give messages to those who dwell on the earth. I would like to give messages and be an "angel" for those who dwell on the earth.

Now a STAR, when you think about it, is also an acronym for Speaking Truth and Righteousness. In this case, instead of this being a podcast, I would like to think that this is a STAR Project - DTG Ministries (the Deep Things of God Ministries), speaking truth and righteousness to those who dwell on the earth. So, laugh at me; say what you will, but I like the idea of a STAR Project, so I'm going to put a section on my website for "STAR Projects," and it's going to be these little studies that we do that connect to teach the gospel.

Now, today, this STAR Project is dealing with INIQUITY. You could say the GOSPEL and INIQUITY, but the entire Bible has a lot to say about iniquity. If you're anything like me (I should say how I was), you're probably thinking, well, INIQUITY is just sin. BUT it isn't.

There is a difference between SIN and INIQUITY. INIQUITY is the thought you have that leads to sin. SIN is just simply the **action of INIQUITY**. It's a big difference.

Thoughts produce feelings. Feelings move you to action; so that first thought - you can't speak it, or do it, unless you think it. It has to be in your mind first, so INIQUITY creates feeling; the feeling moves you to the action; and the idea of Christianity is to catch that iniquity. **Stop the iniquity from going any further than just a thought.**

You know, I've heard it said you can't prevent a bird from flying over your head, but you **can** prevent it from making a nest in your hair. I'm from Oklahoma, and that speaks a lot to me, so think about it; that is a truth that I believe God would have us understand.

Now, if you turn with me to *Exodus, Chapter 34*, I want to show you how the Lord has put this thought/feeling/action into play. In *Exodus, Chapter 34*, I'm going to start reading verse *6*.

Exo 34:6 And the LORD passed by before him, and proclaimed, The LORD, The LORD God, merciful and gracious, longsuffering, and abundant in goodness and truth,

Exo 34:7 Keeping mercy for thousands, forgiving [h5375-lifting up] *iniquity and transgression* [h6588-rebellion] *and sin, ...*

Now, stop there and notice I have numbers beside some of these words. Before I go any further, what do the numbers represent? The numbers come from Strong's Greek and Hebrew Concordance. James Strong, in 1890, published his Strong's Concordance. He took every word in the Bible and gave it a number so that people like you and I (maybe you've never studied Hebrew or Greek), someone like us can come along and read a verse and look up any word in that verse. James Strong will tell you what it means. He will give you the definition taken from Greek and Hebrew. It's one of the most valuable tools that you'll ever have in your Bible study. There are a series of books that use the Strong's numbers. There are Bibles you can get that already have the Strong's number in the Bible itself; every word will have a Strong's number to point you to the definition.

Why is that important? I, for one, got tired of people telling me… I mean, we would be doing a study, and somebody would say, "Well, the Greek says," and "Well, that isn't what it says in the Hebrew." I heard someone say one time, "I may have never studied Greek and Hebrew; maybe I don't know it, but I sure have some dandy books that will help me."

God has given us these tools. You can get the Strong's Concordance for a King James and for a NIV. I don't know of any other version that is numbered to Strong's but the NIV and the King James (whichever one you are using). If you get a Strong's, when I give you a definition, you can look it up and see that I'm not making this up. You can look it up for yourself and not rely on me and be at my mercy to tell you the truth. I've never liked that, and I can't understand why everybody doesn't already have these books. Let's go back to *Exodus 34*. *Exodus 34,* looking at verse 7:

Exo 34:7 Keeping mercy for thousands, forgiving [h5375-lifting up] …

For the word *forgiving,* you'll see a Hebrew number beside it: a Strong's number for the Hebrew. That word is not *to forgive,* it means "to lift up." He will lift up iniquity and transgression. The word is not to forgive, it means to "lift up." *He will lift up iniquity and transgression* **[h6588-rebellion]** *and sin...*

The word *"transgression"* has a Strong's number of **h6588**. It literally means rebellion and sin. So, what do we have? **Iniquity, rebellion, and sin. Thought/feeling/action**. Iniquity – the **thought**, that when you act on it, it becomes **sin**.

Get a concordance and look it up for yourself. What we're seeing here is that **SIN BEGINS IN YOUR MIND,** and when he says he "lifts up iniquity, rebellion, and sin," that is lifting it up from YOU, from your **mind** – from your **thinking**. Let me show you where this comes into play. Turn with me to *Psalms 32,* Starting at verse 1:

Psa 32:1 Blessed is he whose transgression **[h6588-rebellion]** *is forgiven* **[h5375-lifted up]***, whose sin is covered.*

Psa 32:2 Blessed is the man unto whom the LORD imputes not iniquity, and in whose spirit there is no guile.

Now, I want you to drop down to *verse 5*. It says:

Psa 32:5 I acknowledged my sin unto thee, and mine iniquity have I not hid. I said, I will confess my transgressions **[h6588-rebellion or my feeling]** *unto the LORD, and thou forgave* **[h5375-lifted up]** *the iniquity of my sin.*

So, when He lifts up the **iniquity** of your sin, that is **out of your MIND.** In other words, for him to lift up **iniquity**, he is going to give you the truth. He is going to **cleanse** you from that **thought.** There's another place I want to turn to. This is in the New Testament. Turn with me in your Bibles to *1 John, Chapter 1*, reading from verse 9:

1John 1:9 If we confess our sins, he is faithful and just to forgive us our sins, and to cleanse us from all unrighteousness **[g93-iniquity]**.

What do you think that word is? That's **INIQUITY.** He will **cleanse** you from all **INIQUITY**; you confess your sin and he'll cleanse you from the iniquity. That's what we want. We want to be cleansed from the THOUGHT that is moving us to sin!

Now, an example. Let's say that your spouse comes home late - three or four hours late and your first thought when they haven't come home is they're having an affair. See? That **thought is iniquity.** Love will bear all things, hope all things, believe all things, be long suffering, be patient. But to just jump to the conclusion they must be having an affair – that's **INIQUITY.** That **thought is going to create in you a FEELING** - a feeling of anger or jealousy, like the Bible put - 'rebellion' against that person. So when they walk through the door, the way you approach them and what you say to them - **your attitude toward them will be based on the iniquity that was in your mind.** Who knows what you might say or do? Whereas, if you're walking in love, maybe you would meet them at the door and say, "Did you have a wreck or did you have a flat tire? What happened? Are you okay? Can I help you?" There are a thousand different ways to address that issue, but **to allow INIQUITY to control your life – that leads to SIN. This is significant, because there is something I want you to see about Jesus Christ.** Paul wrote this; it's *Titus 2:14.*

Tit 2:14 Who gave himself for us, that he might redeem us from all iniquity, and purify unto himself a peculiar people, zealous of good works.

And since we're looking at the writings of Paul,

2Ti 2:19 Nevertheless the foundation of God stands sure, having this seal, The Lord knows them that are his. And, Let every one that names the name of Christ depart from iniquity.

Christ gave himself to redeem us from iniquity. Now, notice what he DIDN'T say. **He did NOT say he DIED TO PAY YOUR SIN DEBT**.

According to *Titus 2:14*, he died to KEEP YOU FROM SIN. He redeems you from iniquity and if you're in Christ, if you're a Christian walking with Christ, then **you WILL depart from all iniquity.** Think about it. WHY does that even matter? Let's turn and look at one more verse: This one is in *Matthew 7:21*.

Mat 7:21 Not every one that saith unto me, Lord, Lord, shall enter into the kingdom of heaven; but he that doeth the will of my Father which is in heaven. [You want to walk in obedience and do the will of God.]

Mat 7:22 Many will say to me in that day, Lord, Lord, have we not prophesied in thy name? and in thy name have cast out devils? And in thy name done many wonderful works?

Mat 7:23 And then will I profess unto them, I never knew you: depart from me, ye that work iniquity.

Who would say that we've done many wonderful things in your name; we've cast out devils in your name; we've done many wonderful works, but believers? Christians would say that.

But he says, "I never knew you." See, the people who are going to enter heaven are those who do the will of God. **If you're a believer, if you're a Christian, you will depart from all iniquity. He died to give you the ability to depart from INIQUITY.**

And when the day comes, he will say, "Depart from me, ye workers of iniquity." So, at this point, if you're a Christian, if you're going to church somewhere and you happen to get hold of this study and you're looking at it, considering all of the doctrines you've been told - I want you to consider this: I've simply read verses to you. I'm not making anything up. I've simply taken the verses of the Bible and read them to you to show you that **God gives you a way out of your iniquity. You can come to him and confess your sin; confess the rebellion; confess the iniquity. He will lift up that iniquity. He will cleanse you from all unrighteousness,** but who has ever told you to do that?

You know, when I was going to the denominational churches, I would sin and repent; sin and repent; sin and repent. It just went on and on, and I wondered if the Holy Spirit leaves me every time I sin. You know, what's going on here?

I want you to consider what we've read together from the scripture, and in our next installment of our **STAR Projects,** we're going to look at where iniquity comes from and I want you to see – begin to see how Christ deals with this at the cross. **The cross is so much more than just having your sin forgiven! It gives you the ability to overcome sin. When it says that he will save his people from their sin,** I was only told, "Oh, he'll forgive you." Well, it means more than that – **he DIED to REDEEM you from the INIQUITY** and to give you the ability to turn and think in another direction and walk in the righteousness of God.

The next installment of the STAR Projects will deal with "**Where does iniquity come from?**"

INIQUITY PART B
THE AUTHOR OF INIQUITY
Where Does Iniquity Come From?

The Deep Things of God Ministries, "Speaking Truth and Righteousness" equates to a STAR Project. This is the second installment of our project on iniquity - the doctrine of iniquity. In our previous study, I talked about being able to look these words up for yourself. If you could find a Strong's Concordance (where James Strong gave a number to every word in the Bible), when you're studying your Bible, you can look up that verse/word and see what it means according to the Greek and Hebrew. It's really a valuable tool. You can get that free if you get a digital copy.

If you download the E-Sword App, it gives you Bibles; it gives you the Strong's Concordance; it gives you Lexicons and Maps. It's all free, except the NIV. But the King James and the Lexicon, King James and Strong's Concordance - the King James numbered to Strong's... everything you need is right there. It's free, and it is a very valuable tool. I would encourage you to use it.

In our last study, we looked at iniquity; how thoughts produce feelings, feelings move you to action and sin is the action of iniquity. In this study, I want to take it another step, and I want to ask the question: "Where exactly does iniquity come from?" To show you this, I'm going to ask you to turn to *Genesis, Chapter 3*.

Gen 3:1 Now the serpent was more subtil than any beast of the field which the LORD God had made. And he said unto the woman, Yea, hath God said, Ye shall not eat of every tree of the garden?

Gen 3:2 And the woman said unto the serpent, We may eat of the fruit of the trees of the garden:

Gen 3:3 But of the fruit of the tree which is in the midst of the garden, God hath said, Ye shall not eat of it, neither shall ye touch it, lest ye die.

Gen 3:4 And the serpent said unto the woman, Ye shall not surely die:

Gen 3:5 For God doth know that in the day ye eat thereof, then your eyes shall be opened, and ye shall be as gods, knowing good and evil.

What you're seeing is **iniquity** in action. God had given a command and the serpent took the command and twisted it, causing Adam and Eve to fall. When I say he twisted it, that is what iniquity is to me. It is **twisted thinking.** It is something that we devise ourselves instead of listening to God and allowing his righteousness or his understanding to have its way in our hearts.

Because we see this, and we've taken this step, I want to ask you to turn to *1John 3:8.*

1Jn 3:8 He that committeth sin is of the devil; for the devil sins from the beginning. For this purpose the Son of God was manifested, that he might destroy the works of the devil.

Now honestly, when you watch the news or when you look at what's going on in the world, do you see the works of the devil destroyed? The answer is no, you don't, so what does John mean that **"he came to destroy the works of the devil"**? We see in *Genesis 3,* **the works of the devil deal with iniquity, with our twisted thinking**. Let's look at another verse. This one is in *Romans, Chapter 3, verse 22.*

Rom 3:22 Even the righteousness of God which is by [or through] *faith **of** Jesus Christ …*

If your Bible does not have the word "OF" right there, it's wrong. If it says faith "IN" Jesus Christ, it's wrong. It literally is the faith **OF** Christ … *the righteousness of God, which is through the faith OF Jesus Christ* **UNTO** *all and it's* **UPON** *all them that believe; for there's no difference.*

Notice the righteousness of God, through the faith of Christ, is offered UNTO all, but it's only UPON the <u>one who believes</u>. So, when you see the work of the devil being destroyed, you're SEEING that it is destroyed in an individual. It isn't corporate; it doesn't cover everybody. It's only unto the ones who believe. **God's righteousness is HIS understanding.** When you receive his understanding, you are replacing your iniquity. By receiving his understanding, he is redeeming you from iniquity. It's something that happens as you take the time; you study the Bible; you learn the truth. Remember, your faith: Faith **is not** a verb - it is **always** a noun. It is something you have.

Romans 10 – Faith comes by hearing; hearing by the word of God. How shall they hear without a preacher? (Romans 10:17, 14) Faith is something that is taught to you. You believe it and it will replace the way you looked at it before. It will replace the **iniquity**. So, let's go back to *1John 3:4*.

1John 3:4 Whosoever committeth sin transgresses also the law: for sin is the transgression of the law.

A more literal translation of this is: whosoever commits **"the sin"** iniquity also: for **"the sin" is iniquity**.

John right here, has given us a very valuable tool so that we can understand the scripture. When he (John) puts the definite article, the word "the" before "sin," he says it's <u>iniquity</u>. "THE sin" is iniquity. John will do this, and Paul will do this. You'll find this throughout the New Testament, where these men will put the definite article "the" before the word "sin," and you can just come along and say, according to *1John 3:4*, that's iniquity. It's interesting that *1John 3:4* has the word "law" in it twice, but it isn't there at all in the original manuscripts – but by searching, by looking these words up, we discover a powerful tool that helps us understand the Bible. <u>The SIN</u> is **INIQUITY.** I want to take this back to *1John* and read that verse again and continue so you can see what he says:

1John 3:4 Whosoever committeth sin transgresses also the law: for sin is the transgression of the law. [Actually reads: *Whosoever commits "the sin" iniquity also: for "the sin" is iniquity.* Now, remember, SIN is the <u>action</u> of iniquity.]

1John 3:5 And ye know that he was manifested to take away our sins; and in him is no sin.

1John 3:6 Whosoever abides [remains] *in him sins not* [does not sin]: *whosoever sins hath not seen him, neither* [or] *known him.*

1John 3:7 Little children, let no man deceive you: he that doeth righteousness is righteous, even as he is righteous.

1John 3:8 He that committeth sin is of the devil [He that commits "the" sin - (now here it is) - he who commits iniquity is of the devil]; *for the devil sins from the beginning. For this purpose the Son of God was manifested, that he might destroy the works of the devil.*

Now does that make any more sense to you, since you see where iniquity comes from? Christ came to destroy the works of the devil. What he did, what he said, the power he gives you is offered to everybody, but it is only going to be upon those who believe it. <u>He died - he gave himself to redeem us from iniquity</u>. In so doing, he destroys the work of the devil in you. Let's turn and look at one more verse. This is in the *Gospel of John, Chapter 8.*

John 8:30 As he spoke these words, many believed on him.

John 8:31 Then said Jesus to those Jews which believed on him [He is not talking to unbelievers. These people did believe], *If ye continue in my word, then are ye my disciples indeed;*

John 8:32 And ye shall know the truth, and the truth shall make you free.

John 8:33 They answered him, We be Abraham's seed, and were never in bondage to any man: how sayest thou, Ye shall be made free?

John 8:34 Jesus answered them, Verily, verily, I say unto you, Whosoever committeth sin ["**the**" sin] *is the servant of sin* ["**the**" sin].

Now remember, the same guy who wrote *1John* wrote the *Gospel of John* and HE says in *1John 3:4*, that he's talking about iniquity. Whosoever commits **iniquity** <u>is a servant of iniquity</u>.

John 8:35 And the servant abides not in the house for ever: but the Son abides ever.

John 8:36 If the Son therefore shall make you free, ye shall be free indeed.

Again, remember what we read in *Matthew 7* - that the people said, "We've prophesied in your name. We've done many wonderful works in your name; we've cast out devils in your name." And he said, "But I never knew you. You're a worker of iniquity." Here he spoke to the Jews who believed: "Now if you continue in my word..." Do you know why he would say "If you continue in my word"? Because what I'm teaching you right now isn't something you get at the beginning of your walk with Christ.

It took <u>years</u> for me to see this truth and to recognize the death of Christ and what was really happening on that cross. That is why I felt such an urgency to do these projects, the first one being iniquity, because I see people floundering in their churches, and I see people who do not seem to have the ability to overcome sin; why? Because they don't understand iniquity and they don't understand what God has given us through the cross to help us turn from, *to <u>resist</u> the devil and he will flee from you (James 4:7)*. Well, that's your iniquity that he's talking about.

Christ died to give us this. He died to redeem you from iniquity. I decided that I could not live my life ignoring that. The man gave his life and it's my prayer that not a single thing about that cross be wasted by me. I want to see it. I want to know it, and I want it applied to my heart. I want to be free. If he says that the Son will make you free from iniquity, I believe it.

I believe it, and I'm going to show you how that works. I'm going to show you the meaning of the cross and how the Son of God redeems us from all iniquity. Remember what we read in the last study - if you're in Christ, you **will separate**; you **will depart from all iniquity.**

INIQUITY PART C
THE DOUBLE

Hi, I'm Scott Stanley, and this is the third installment of a STAR PROJECT on iniquity. I decided to record some studies that would simplify the Bible, and the first subject I felt impressed to do was iniquity. Now, as these studies go out, more and more people listen to them and I'm getting feedback from people asking questions. They want to know what I mean about this and that, and I welcome any questions. You can contact me via email, phone, or text. It's easier if you call, but I'll try to text you insofar as I understand.

One question that I have received deals with the word "iniquity" - how do we even know iniquity is a thought and not an action? How do we know it's "thought"? *Matthew, Chapter 15* - Christ makes a statement there, and I don't know that people really grasp the meaning of what he is saying.

Mat 15:16 And Jesus said, Are ye also yet without understanding?

Mat 15:17 Do not ye yet understand, that whatsoever enters in at the mouth goes into the belly, and is cast out into the draught?

Mat 15:18 But those things which proceed out of the mouth come forth from the heart; and they defile the man.

Mat 15:19 For out of the heart proceed evil thoughts, ...

Now, he is going to list these evil thoughts. I want you to consider he isn't saying that out of the mouth comes evil thought and also this and this and this; he's going to define the evil thought.

Mat 15:19 For out of the heart proceed evil thoughts, murders, adulteries, fornications, thefts, false witness, blasphemies:

Mat 15:20 These are the things which defile a man: but to eat with unwashen hands defiles not [doesn't defile] *a man.*

What if we were having a discussion and the word "murder" was brought up, and I were to say to you, "Oh, murder - well, that's an evil thought"? And maybe you would reply, "Well, you know it's actually more than that - murder is when you kill somebody." And I would say, "But it's an evil thought." Jesus just said that. I'm not making it up. Out of the mouth, out of the heart come evil thoughts, murder.

How would you apply the word iniquity to this? Is iniquity something you do or something you think? Murder comes from the heart. Adultery comes from the heart. Fornication - it comes out of the heart. When I read this, iniquity, i.e., literally killing somebody, it starts in the heart. If you call murder, the literal murder, iniquity, you have to call the evil thoughts iniquity. It makes more sense to me that **God is trying to help us stop sin in its tracks in order to save us from our sins.** If all he is doing is giving you forgiveness for following through on the evil thought, that basically is the Christianity I grew up with.

I believe I have graduated to something that helps me in my life, and sets me free from "**the sin**" – **INIQUITY!**

The action of iniquity is sin, and that is the way I would consider murder, fornication, and adultery. BUT I feel like this is proof enough that **INIQUITY is THE EVIL THOUGHT**. Again, he is calling murder an evil thought; it isn't just a sin. It has to start in the mind. **Everything** you do or say **must** begin in the mind. This really leads me to the study for today.

Each study progressively gets deeper, and today is no exception. I want to use this verse we've just read. What you're looking at is literal/spiritual. Spiritual is "of the mind." Murder, adultery, and theft all begin in the mind. So, let's take iniquity and move to the cross. I pray we take our time doing this and that no one is stumbling over what I'm saying. It's essential that we move to the cross, because he gave himself to redeem us from all iniquity. **The purpose of the cross was to redeem you from iniquity.**

Isa 40:1 Comfort ye, comfort ye my people, saith your God.

Isa 40:2 Speak ye comfortably [to the heart] *to Jerusalem, and cry unto her, that her warfare is accomplished, that her iniquity is pardoned: for she hath received of the LORD'S hand double for all her sins.*

When you begin to lust after a woman, or you get really angry at somebody (where you could just ruin their lives), you could just murder them - if you're a Christian, the warfare has begun. The warfare is happening in your heart. Maybe you're married, maybe you have children and you begin to be attracted to someone, and you realize in your heart, "I know this is wrong, and I'm fighting it with all my might." The warfare has started. But in this verse, he is saying to speak to the heart, that the warfare and the struggling, **the iniquity - it's over**.

Speak to the heart and say *your warfare is accomplished, the iniquity is pardoned*. A better word for **pardoned** is **reconciled** in this verse. That is what I want all of us to experience in our lives – victory. But notice what he says and how you receive the victory.

Isa 40:2 Speak ye comfortably [Speak to the heart] *to Jerusalem, and cry unto her, that her warfare is accomplished, that her iniquity is pardoned* [Why?]: *for she hath received of the LORD'S hand double for all her sins.*

Two things:

1) *The righteousness of God is **unto** everyone, but only **upon** those who believe (Romans 3:22)*. You have your victory because you received something. **You received it, and you believed it.** It was taught to you, and you received it into your heart, **setting you free**.

2) Here he calls it the **"double,"** and I must ask the question - have you ever heard of the double before? Is this the first time you've ever heard that **"if I can receive the double, I'll have victory in my Christian Life"**? What is the double? To simplify this as much as I possibly can, the double is what we were discussing, looking at the word iniquity. There is a literal and spiritual meaning to the things Christ taught. He even said this. Do you remember in *Matthew Chapter 5 (Matt 5:21-32)* he said, *"You have been told, 'thou shalt not kill.' I tell you, don't even get angry. You've been told, 'you shall not commit adultery.' I tell you don't lust. If you lust in your heart, you're already guilty."*

You take that **outward** commandment of *Thou shalt not kill*, and you put it **inward**. If you are not going to kill, Jesus said don't even get angry - don't let that even begin. Remember, you can't stop the bird from flying over your head, but you can prevent it from building a nest.

So, **Christ took the law and put it inward -** he applied it inwardly. So maybe if you look at this law outward, maybe you think you're doing okay because you haven't killed anybody. You haven't committed adultery, but **have you been angry**? And **have you lusted**? Yes, but the law says not to kill. Jesus shifted gears on that understanding. Paul wrote something very significant regarding this and it's in *Romans 7:14.*

Rom 7:14 For we know that the law is spiritual: but I am carnal, sold under sin.

If you are carnal and you don't understand spiritual things, then **you do not understand the law, and that is where the Jews were. THEY DID NOT UNDERSTAND THE LAW WAS SPIRITUAL.** Again, *Romans 7:14* makes the statement, *"the law is spiritual."* And you know what? **It always was.** In God's heart, he would never have you live your life in lust or live your life in hate, anger, and bitterness.

So, when he said, *"Thou shalt not kill,"* Jesus informs us that means **don't get angry**. That's what that actually means. **DON'T EVEN GO IN THAT DIRECTION.**

That was enlightening for me. It was like, wow, I never really thought of that! It makes more sense that **God is saving us inwardly**. Why did Christ die? To **redeem you from iniquity.** This is part of the **iniquity I have carried all my life**. What I was taught about keeping the Ten Commandments, no one put that within (applying it to the mind, the heart) and really taught me how to overcome the inward. **IT IS THE CROSS WHERE YOU ARE REDEEMED FROM INIQUITY.** So, when he says your warfare is accomplished - your iniquity is reconciled, **he's talking about at the cross** - that's where that happened.

If you do not understand the cross, you're not going to be redeemed from the iniquity of your mind. Just like we read in

Matthew 7:22-23: Haven't we done many wonderful things? Haven't we cast out demons? Haven't we prophesied in your name? Depart from me. You are a worker of iniquity.

You're working your iniquity. Iniquity is the thought (the genesis of sin); the action of it, or the works of it is sin. You may think everything is fine because you haven't done this, and you haven't done that. But **you haven't understood the cross and your warfare is not accomplished. YOU STILL HAVE YOUR INIQUITY**. We need to go to the cross and correct this, and that's where we're headed. We're headed to Calvary.

INIQUITY PART D
THE CROSS

This is the fourth installment of a STAR Project on INIQUITY. Let's start with a short recap of what we've covered.

We've seen that there is a **difference between iniquity and sin. Sin is the action of iniquity.** We've seen that the devil originates the iniquity and Christ was manifested to destroy the works of the devil. *(1 John 3:8)* Christ gave himself to redeem us from all iniquity. In the last study, we saw **"the double,"** how *Isaiah 40:2* tells us that *your warfare is accomplished, your iniquity is pardoned because you've received "the double."* We saw the double was more of a spiritual/literal thing. When we read the scripture, it's full of literal truth, but I've learned that there is always a spiritual lesson that goes with the story. I wanted to add another verse about "the double." This is in *Job 11:6.*

Job 11:6 And that he would shew thee the secrets of wisdom, that they are double to that which is! Know therefore that God exacts of thee less than thine iniquity deserves. [God exacts less of you than your iniquity deserves.]

The double, the wisdom of God, is double to that which is. This is what we've been saying, **you look at the law - you've been told not to kill. What it means is don't even get angry**. There's always the literal "don't kill," but there's a spiritual meaning to it. Turn to *Isaiah 53*:6. I want to show you something that's been there for 2,000 years.

Isa 53:6 All we like sheep have gone astray; we have turned everyone to his own way; and the LORD hath laid on him the iniquity of us all.

Now that we have **iniquity** fresh in our minds, does that say something different to you now? I've always read that as 'he laid on him our sin,' and I've heard preachers say, "the sin of the whole world was put on Christ," **yet I can't find a single verse that says that!** *Isaiah 53: 6 - the Lord laid on him the iniquity of us all.* **Iniquity is "thought."** We saw that in *Matthew 15*. Evil thoughts proceed from the heart - murder, adultery; those are evil thoughts; and he laid on Christ the iniquity of us all. This has to be what Paul is referring to in *2 Corinthians 5:21*.

2Co 5:21 For he hath made him to be sin for us, who knew no sin [He who knew no sin, was made to be sin for us]*; that we might be made the righteousness of God in him.*

He knew no sin. How do you take somebody who doesn't know sin and make him **to be sin**? When you compare the verses, *the Lord laid on him the INIQUITY of us all,* what could God have possibly done to show the iniquity of the whole world? I look at myself - I live now 2,000 years after the cross. **How could my iniquity be put on him when I didn't even exist?** How does that work? Because God used "the double." Again remember, your warfare is accomplished. *Your iniquity is reconciled, because you received the double (Isa 40:2).* **There was a spiritual meaning behind what was literally happening to Christ.**

Let's talk about sin: there are two kinds of sin. To simplify this - there are the things that you have done to other people and there are things that they have done to you. **What YOU have done to other people creates guilt. What other people have done TO YOU creates anger, bitterness, and wrath.** On the cross, Christ was wearing a crown of thorns - that is a symbol of our guilt. A crown of thorns equals those things that come up in your mind - you remember the things you've done, and it just pricks your mind. It's hard for you to even recall those things because it bothers you. **That's a crown of thorns. So, God used "the double." The crown of thorns equals your guilt.** Whose guilt? Everybody on the planet has guilt and has worn that crown of thorns.

What about the stripes on his back? There wasn't a single stripe on his back that he did to himself. It **all** happened **TO** him, and **the stripes on his back equal those things that people have done to you throughout your life, and you just can't get over it.** You just can't forgive them for it - whether it's an ex-wife or a husband or children or parents. **The things people have done to you have put stripes on your back.** Your back is a symbol of where you carry your burden, so **the stripes on his back, that is "the double."** It is a symbol of the pain that we carry from what has happened. His nakedness: you're either going to be clothed with the righteousness of God or be naked. **Naked is when you expose yourself, and you think your own thoughts; you do your own thing. You act on your iniquity.**

There was yet another symbol and that was when the land turned dark. *(Mark 15:33)* **Four symbols: 1) your crown of thorns, 2) stripes on your back, 3) your nakedness, and 4) your darkness.** When you're in darkness, it's because you don't know God. God is light *(1John 1:5)*. In those four things, again, looking at the **"the double"** and **realizing you've received the double - so your iniquity is reconciled.**

Four things - **each one is caused by iniquity:** 1) The crown of thorns – your guilt (what you have done to others that prick your conscience); 2) The stripes on your back – your unwillingness to forgive what others have done to you. Maybe you're just unable to forgive because of the iniquity, the way you're looking at it; 3) Your nakedness – you expose yourself when you display anger, lust, and your own ideas and 4) The darkness of the land - you're in darkness because you're not clothed with his righteousness, because you don't know him. What you're seeing on the cross **is a picture of the soul of every person on this planet** and when Jesus died, he was made to be sin. **He who knew no sin was made to be sin. God did not lay on him your sin. He laid on him your iniquity.**

THE CROSS DEPICTS THE SOUL OF ALL HUMANITY WITHOUT CHRIST!

Another picture is the serpent on the pole.

John 3:14 And as Moses lifted up the serpent in the wilderness, even so must the Son of man be lifted up: [Remember, the serpent is where iniquity comes from.]

There is a reason for this. It's to deliver us, save us from iniquity. Turn to *Romans 3:21*.

Rom 3:21 But now the righteousness of God without the law is manifested [to us], *being witnessed by the law and the prophets;* [The law and the prophets spoke of this]

Rom 3:22 Even the righteousness of God which is by [through the] *faith of Jesus Christ unto all and upon all them that believe: for there is no difference:*

Rom 3:23 For all have sinned, and come short of the glory of God;

Rom 3:24 Being justified freely by his grace through the redemption that is in Christ Jesus: [and remember the redemption of Christ is to be redeemed from iniquity]

Rom 3:25 Whom God hath set forth to be a propitiation [that word propitiation right there would be better translated as 'an act of mercy'] *through faith in his blood* [or in his death], *to declare his righteousness* [to declare as you have faith in his blood - God is declaring his righteousness for what?] *for the remission* {g3929 passing over} *of sins that are past, through the forbearance of God;* [for the passing over of your past sin which he did in his forbearance]

How does the cross do that? Did you understand what he said? Through the blood of Christ or through his death, God is declaring his righteousness for passing over your past sin. Why would he pass over your past sin? Can you go to the cross and see where he is declaring why he would pass over your past sin? The very first thing that Christ said on that cross was, *"Father forgive them for they know not what they do."* *(Luke 23:34)* SO, what happened? Christ was not making a record of what these people were doing to him. They were murdering him and in the midst of it, *"Father forgive them for they know not what they do."* Not one of those men repented. None of them prayed "the prayer."

No one asked God to forgive them, but they were forgiven.

Now I've got a question for you: If Christ would do that for the people killing him, why wouldn't he do that for you and me?

All of your life, God has passed over your past sins. He has done that all of your life. Why? Because you don't know what you're doing. But what's making you do that? Iniquity. *Sin is the action of iniquity.* If you don't understand iniquity and how to put that away, God is saying you don't really know what you're doing. The person who does know what he's doing is the person who understands the truth.

We have people calling themselves Christians and yet when you say, "Well, why did he die?" ... "Well, he died to pay your sin debt." I cannot find that verse in the Bible. **I see he died to redeem you from all iniquity; God laid on him the iniquity of us all.**

Who puts your sin on Christ? **YOU do that.** When you look at the Old Testament - they would slaughter an animal, they would put their hand on the head of that animal. Hands are a symbol of your works and that is a picture of you coming to God like he said in *1John 1: 9, confess your sin, and he's faithful and just to forgive you your sin.* But he's going to also cleanse you of that iniquity. *Blessed is the man to whom the Lord will not impute iniquity. (Psa 32:2)*

God didn't put your sin on him. **YOU do that** when you come before him, fall on your knees and cry out for forgiveness. He would say, "You know, you didn't know what you were doing, but I forgive you and I'm going to cleanse you from that iniquity." What you're hearing right now, I know, is radical, but **why** is it radical? Because this is not what mainstream churches teach you. They teach you, or at least what I was taught, you sin and repent, sin and repent, sin and repent; and when he gives you a new body, you'll be okay. You'll quit sinning when he gives you a new body, yet **everything originates in the mind.** What he is trying to do is renew your mind. **The renewing of the mind is what you want in your life.**

Remember where he said that the perfection of your faith, the completion of your faith is the salvation of your soul? *(1Pe 1:9) The completion {g5056 completion} of your faith is the salvation of your soul.*

I've had people argue with me that when they pray "the prayer," they're saved, and yet what does it mean *to work out your own salvation with fear and trembling? (Php 2:12)* We've already read he died to redeem you from iniquity. He was manifest to destroy the works of the devil. Your warfare is accomplished. Your iniquity is reconciled when you receive the double. I'm just simply here to tell you that when you go to that cross, there is more going on there than you've ever understood before.

You've got to SEE your INIQUITY. When he forgives the people killing him, why can't you accept the fact that **God has passed over your sin and he is forgiving you?** You need to be cleansed of the twisted, crooked thinking that you've had, **and if he has forgiven you, that means he has forgiven everyone who's hurt you. They're forgiven too.**

So, you see, he lifts away the crown of thorns. He begins to heal your stripes - *by his stripes we're healed*. When you understand what that means, you are healed. **You can be healed from all the people that you were unable to forgive. He clothes you with his understanding of righteousness, and he takes away the darkness by showing you the only true and living God.**

1John 4: 8 God is love. Love is defined in *1Corinthians 13*, and in verse 5 he states *LOVE DOES NOT MAKE A RECORD OF SIN.* **Why would God lay on Christ the sin of the world when God doesn't even make a record of it?** Why? **Christ declares from the cross why God passed over your sin.** It's because **you don't know what you're doing.** You never understood **the ROOT of your sin is INIQUITY.**

These are some heavy things to consider, and I know it's a completely different direction than you've ever thought before. I would beg you to pray about it. Look at the scriptures. We haven't done anything but read the scriptures. Seek the Lord for your salvation.

TRINITY PART A
DIVINITY OF CHRIST

Hi, I'm Scott Stanley, founder of DTG Ministries. DTG is an acronym for the "Deep Things of God," and this is a STAR Project. I wanted to do STAR Projects to help people understand some of the deep things of God. One project we've already done was on INIQUITY and I pray if you have not listened to that, you will take the time to go watch those four short videos on INIQUITY because it will help you understand what we're doing today. We're talking about TRINITY.

I feel like the TRINITY has been misunderstood. In fact, let me read a document from the United Methodist Church which was recently sent out to their pastors. Each year the United Methodist Church observes a day called **Trinity Sunday.** (The next paragraph can be found at this link):

https://www.umcdiscipleship.org/worship-planning/living-the-spirit-life/ trinity-sunday-year-c-lectionary-planning-notes.

The first paragraph reads: **A plea is made to the worship teams** *"that you avoid the inclination to try and explain the TRINITY. The church has wrestled with the precise meaning of this theological concept from the very beginning. So freed from the expectation of trying to make sense of the Trinity, worship can be engaged in experiencing the TRINITY. That's where the doctrine comes from anyway, from our experience of God and the experience of God's people from the beginning."* **Last sentence:** *"Our purpose is to expand our experience and understanding of God as we worship together on this day."*

So, please don't try to explain the Trinity, they say. Leave it alone; you'll be inclined to try to explain it. Don't. It doesn't make any sense.

Today, we're going to travel down a path and try to make sense of this. If I were to ask you, "What is the Trinity?" what would YOU say?

I tried to find a short, concise explanation of the Trinity so I could do this study, and I found one online. **Trinity: There is one God, Father, Son, and Holy Spirit - a unity of three co-eternal persons -The Trinity.** By the time we finish our studies on this project, we're going to have a better understanding of what it is and what it means. You won't have to ask people to explain it because *nobody knows what it is - it's confusing.*

To begin, I want to go to *Genesis 3:15*. This is where Adam and Eve sin and they have been approached by the serpent. We saw in our studies on iniquity that iniquity stems from, or comes from the serpent, the whisperer. So, God is addressing the whisperer.

Gen 3:15 And I will put enmity [hostility] *between thee and the woman, and between thy seed and her seed; it shall bruise thy head* [this hostility will bruise your head], *and thou shalt bruise his heel* [h6119].

My entire Christian life I was told this was a prophecy about Christ - the first Biblical prophecy about the coming of Messiah - and we know from our studies on iniquity:

Titus 2: 14 - he gave himself to redeem us from all iniquity. 1John 3:8 - he was manifest to destroy the works of the devil. So, we see that in this prophecy he would bruise the head of the serpent, but what does it mean **the serpent, or iniquity would bruise the heel of Christ? What is the heel of Christ?** Surely you don't take that literally and think, well, the serpent bruised his heel. Let's turn to *Psalms 89:51*.

Psa 89:51 Wherewith thine enemies have reproached, O LORD; wherewith they have reproached the footsteps [h6119] *of thine anointed.*

The anointed: Ultimately the anointed one is Christ. The word "footsteps" is the same word, "HEEL," used in Genesis 3:15. (I believe the Hebrew number is 6119.) Look it up; it's the **same word**. What does it mean **to bruise the footsteps of the anointed**

one, or of Christ? His heel, the footsteps of Christ for me, would be **the Life of Christ from eternity to his death, to eternity future - the life of Christ**. And you know, without me trying to prove it to you, that **the serpent has twisted and turned all of these truths and facts about the Savior**. Whether we're talking about eternity past, born in Bethlehem, died on the cross - all of these things have been twisted. And, honestly, **If YOU are not making a decided effort to UNDERSTAND what you're being told at church, then YOU MAY BE DECEIVED YOURSELF.**

We can't imagine these pastors, who are our friends and family, purposefully deceiving us. They would not purposefully deceive you, but it could be they don't know the truth either. Perhaps what they're trying to tell you is what they think is the truth. Maybe there is something more to it than you've heard before, and it will begin to make sense to you. So, let's begin this study by looking at **TRINITY**.

We're going to key on the Son of God first. Turn to the *Gospel of John Chapter 1*. Anytime that the divinity of Christ is challenged, this is the verse that people turn to, *John 1:1*.

John 1:1 In the beginning was the Word, and the Word was with God, and the Word was God.

John 1:2 The same was in the beginning with God.

John 1:3 All things were made by him; and without him was not any thing made that was made.

John 1:4 In him was life; and the life was the light of men.

John 1:5 And the light shineth in darkness; and the darkness comprehended it not....

John 1:10 He was in the world, and the world was made by him, and the world knew him not.

Now, honestly, **how could anybody read that and see anything other than the divinity of Christ?** Definitely, no one could take away his divinity. **He was in the beginning with God, he was God, he is God**. He made all things. He became flesh and dwelt among us. Who else could that be talking about? It goes pretty good in this chapter for me, until you come to verse 18.

John 1:18 No man hath seen God at any time; the only begotten Son, which is in the bosom [or in the closest relationship possible] *of the Father, he hath declared him.*

How can you say Jesus is God, Jesus created all things, Jesus was made flesh, and no one's seen God? For me, for years, that just didn't cut it. It's like, "I don't believe there are any contradictions in the Bible, so how can we justify what is being said," **because it SAYS that HE CAME TO DECLARE THE FATHER,** and **NO man has seen God at ANY time?** Let's turn back and get an answer for this by turning to *Exodus 24:9.*

Exo 24:9 Then went up Moses, and Aaron, Nadab, and Abihu, and seventy of the elders of Israel:

Exo 24:10 And they saw the God of Israel: and there was under his feet as it were a paved work of a sapphire stone, and as it were the body of heaven in his clearness.

Exo 24:11 And upon the nobles of the children of Israel he laid not his hand: also they saw God, and did eat and drink.

Again, those statements - how could you take that any other way, except **HERE, we see it's the GOD OF ISRAEL.** Now, **WHO IS THE GOD OF ISRAEL** that they did see? Turn to *Psalms 68*:7-8.

Psa 68:7 O God, when thou went forth before thy people, when thou didst march through the wilderness; Selah:

Psa 68:8 The earth shook, the heavens also dropped at the presence of God: even Sinai itself was moved at the presence of God, the God of Israel.

So, when you look at God coming down on Sinai, **WHO came down on Sinai? THE GOD OF ISRAEL.** *No man had seen God at any time, (John 1:18)* but they **DID SEE the God of Israel** *(Exodus 24:10)* and **IT WAS THE GOD OF ISRAEL** who came down on Sinai and **GAVE THAT LAW.** That is important to understand. Why? Because of what is stated in *Hebrews Chapter 9.*

Heb 9:16 For where a testament [or a covenant] *is, there must also of necessity be the death of the testator.* [Or the one who gave the covenant]

Heb 9:17 For a testament [a covenant] *is of force after men are dead: otherwise it is of no strength at all while the testator lives.*

WHO gave the law? WHO gave the Testament? Jesus Christ. WHO died? It had to be Jesus Christ. **He was the testator. He was the one who gave the covenant.** So, where are we with this? **We have every right to take** *John 1* **and see Jesus Christ as God, as creator, as coming in the flesh. We see Jesus Christ in** *Exodus 24* with Moses, Nadab and Abihu, and the elders. **They SEE the GOD OF ISRAEL. They EAT with the GOD OF ISRAEL.**

Psalm 68 - The **God of Israel** comes down on Sinai and **GIVES THE COVENANT.** *Hebrews 9* - **Therefore, HE HAS TO DIE. HE GAVE THE COVENANT. THAT COVENANT IS OF NO FORCE WITHOUT THE DEATH OF THE TESTATOR.**

So far, **we've done nothing but read the scripture**, and I hope, for you, it's making a little more sense that **Jesus was with God. He is God.** No one has seen God; they've seen the God of Israel and it was the God of Israel who came to declare the Father. *(John 17:26)*

In the next part of this project on the **Trinity,** we will be searching verses about the Father and the Son. We will, through scripture, piece this together, then iron all this out as to the meaning of the Trinity… so we don't look at this and claim that it's all just too deep - that it is too much and it can't be understood. **It IS understandable, and you WILL understand it by the time we finish this project.**

TRINITY PART B
THE HEAD OF CHRIST

Hi. I'm Scott Stanley with DTG Ministries. We are exploring the Deep Things of God.

This is the second installment of the STAR Project on the Trinity. In the first episode (Part A), I shared with you one definition describing the Trinity as being three people: The Father, the Son, and the Holy Spirit – three co-eternal persons. If you look online, you will find several definitions of the Trinity. You'll discover people will say that the **Father/Son/Holy Spirit is "co-divine," "co-equal," "co-substantial," and that there is "one God in three persons."** In today's study, we will examine **"co-equal,"** and in our next episode, we'll explore **"co-eternal."**

Let's begin with *1Corinthians 11:3*.

*1Co 11:3 But I would have you know, that the head of every man is Christ; and the head of the woman is the man; and **the head of Christ is God**.*

That speaks volumes! Why would Paul say that **Christ has a head**? Let me show you something he says in Ephesians.

*Eph 1:3 Blessed be **the God** and Father **of our Lord Jesus Christ**, who hath blessed us with all spiritual blessings in heavenly places in Christ:*

*Eph 1:17 That **the God** of our **Lord Jesus Christ**, the Father of glory, may give unto you the spirit of wisdom and revelation in the knowledge of him:*

That's what we're looking at today, that we would have a spirit of wisdom and revelation in the knowledge of God. *1Peter 1:3…*

1Pe 1:3 Blessed be **the God** *and Father* **of our Lord Jesus Christ**, *which according to his abundant mercy hath begotten us again unto a lively* [living] *hope by the resurrection of Jesus Christ from the dead,*

Christ has a Head. Christ has a Father and Christ has a God. When I read these verses, and then (some of) the Trinity definitions, I think… That doesn't fit. What is it that people can't accept about Jesus Christ being the Son of God? Having a head? Having a God?

Rev 3:12 Him that overcomes will I make a pillar in the temple of **my God** [Now, who is speaking here? This is Jesus Christ, LONG AFTER the resurrection], *and he shall go no more out: and I will write upon him the name of* **my God**, *and the name of the city of* **my God**, *which is new Jerusalem, which cometh down out of heaven from* **my God**: *and I will write upon him my new name.*

Four times in one verse Jesus himself states that HE HAS A GOD, and you know he also said that in *John 20:17.*

John 20:17 Jesus saith unto her, Touch me not; for I am not yet ascended to my Father: but go to my brethren, and say unto them, I ascend unto my Father, and your Father; and to **my God**, *and your God.*

Immediately after the resurrection, he is referring to HIS Father as HIS God.

When the *Book of Revelation* is given, Jesus refers to **having a God**, which **we know is his Father. He has a God.** Let's look at yet another verse, *Hebrews 1:8.* This is the Father to the Son and is a quote from *Psalms 45.*

Heb 1:8 But unto the Son he saith, Thy throne, O God, is for ever and ever: a scepter of righteousness is the scepter of thy kingdom. [Here, we see the Father referring to his Son as God.]

Heb 1:9 Thou hast loved righteousness, and hated iniquity; therefore God, **even thy God**, *hath anointed thee with the oil of gladness above thy fellows.*

The FATHER REFERS TO HIS SON AS GOD, but THE FATHER TELLS HIS SON, "I am YOUR GOD."

If we have in a Trinity definition that the Father and the Son are coequal, then that makes that Trinity definition **false**. If you're going to say that the Father and the Son are co-divine, then that Trinity definition is FALSE AS WELL.

Maybe for some minds I'm raising questions but let me show you another verse. This is in *1 Corinthians 8:6*.

1 Cor 8:6 But to us there is but one God, the Father, of whom are all things, and we in him; and one Lord Jesus Christ, by whom are all things, and we by him.

1 Co 8:7 Howbeit there is not in every man that knowledge: ...

Does Jesus have a God? He does. Does he have a father? He does. **That's his God**. Does he have a head? He does. **That is his Father and his God.** So, if we see in the *Gospel of John Chapter 1*, that Jesus is God, why would Paul say in *1 Corinthians 8: 6* what we just read - *But to us, there is one God the Father*? The best way I can explain that is, at one time in my life, I worked at a print shop, and it was started by a man who turned the shop over to his son. When the son would come into the shop, he was the boss - he was the guy. But, when the father and the son were in the shop together, **we treated them both equally, BUT in their sphere BETWEEN the father and the son, THEY WERE NOT EQUAL.**

This was the father's business and he had turned it over to his son. You would see the father give his son commands - you know, "Go get that ticket," "Give me this," "Bring this over here," that kind of thing. **THE SON WAS SUBJECT TO HIS FATHER.** Between them, the father was the boss, and we on the floor knew that (even though we treated them equally). Now, maybe that's a crude representation of God the Father, and his Son. **Keep in mind that today we're exploring co-equal.** The next time we'll examine co-eternal and what that means. **Jesus refers to his Father as HIS God. The apostles refer to God as the Father *and* God of Jesus.** Paul says **God is the head of Jesus,** so let's look at the *Gospel of John 17:3*. Jesus is praying to God.

John 17:3 And this is life eternal, that they might know thee the only true God, and Jesus Christ, whom thou hast sent.

THAT is even MORE explanatory. That helps us see that, from Jesus Christ to his Father, he refers to him as **the only true God.**

Maybe again, that raises question marks for you. Maybe there are things still yet to be uncovered that will give us more insight. But, in the meantime, **I can't deny what is written in the scripture.** I see people taking the doctrine of the Trinity and making more out of it by putting their own meanings to it. **I believe the scriptures are plain - that the Father and the Son are NOT co-equal.**

Let's go back to the *Gospel of John 1:1* – This is kind of where we started with Part A of the Trinity Project.

John 1:1 In the beginning, was the Word, and the Word was with God, and the Word was God.

There is a word the King James left out here, and most Bibles do. It's the definite article; it is the word **"the,"** and it is before the word "God." Here's the way this reads:

John 1:1 In the beginning was the Word, and the Word was with **[the]** *God, and the Word was God.*

John 1:2 The same was in the beginning with **[the]** *God.*

In two places in the *Gospel of John* (the very beginning of the first two verses) **they left out the word THE, making a distinction between the Word OF God and THE God.** We already see the Word is Jesus Christ - he's the God of Israel. He is divine. But, according to the apostles and Christ and the Father, **he, himself, HAS a God,** and **he IS NOT co-equal with the Father.**

1Co 15:22 For as in Adam all die, even so in Christ shall all be made alive.

1Co 15:23 But every man in his own order: Christ the firstfruits; afterward they that are Christ's at his coming.

1Co 15:24 Then cometh the end, when he shall have delivered up the kingdom to God, even the Father; when he shall have put down all rule and all authority and power.

1Co 15:25 For he must reign, till he hath put all enemies under his feet.

1Co 15:26 The last enemy that shall be destroyed is death.

1Co 15:27 For he hath put all things under his feet. But when he saith all things are put under him, it is manifest that he is excepted, which did put all things under him. [It means everyone EXCEPT the one who did put all things under him - the Father.]

1Co 15:28 And when all things shall be subdued unto him, then shall the Son also himself be subject unto him that put all things under him, [so] *that God may be all in all.*

That is quite a few scriptures - because **we're talking about the end of the world**. We're talking about the end **when the kingdom is delivered to the Father.** *Psalms 110:1, The Father is to put all things under the feet of Christ.* This verse *(Psalms 110:1)*, is the most quoted Old Testament verse in the New Testament. **The FATHER is putting all things under the feet of the Son.** When he does, the kingdom will be delivered to God and **the Son will be SUBJECT to his Father.**

Would you say the Father and Son are co-equal? Hopefully not. Hopefully, you are beginning to see the co-equal part of the Trinity doctrine begins to break down. **The scriptures DESTROY that concept.**

TRINITY PART C
THE WISDOM OF GOD

Hi. I'm Scott Stanley with DTG Ministries and we are going to continue exploring the Deep things of God today. This is the third installment of our STAR Project on the Trinity, and I think by the time we finish, you will gain a better understanding of me and where I'm coming from because the word "Trinity," the concept of the Trinity (that I hear from the churches) has plagued me for years **because there are so many verses in the Bible that seem to contradict what the churches say the Trinity means**. No one is denying the Father-Son-Holy Spirit, but it's **the definition** the churches give the Trinity that is hard for me to cope with using the scriptures. Years ago, I read a verse in *1 Corinthians* which has to do with Christ being the wisdom of God.

1 Co 1:24 But unto them which are called, both Jews and Greeks, Christ the power of God, <u>and the wisdom of God</u>.

What makes that so significant, is that there is a chapter, *Proverbs 8*, where wisdom is personified. In other words, these verses speak of the *wisdom of God* as if it were a person. When I saw this in *1 Corinthians 1*, *Christ is the wisdom of God*, the first thought I had was, **"Can I go to *Proverbs 8* and see Christ in it?"**

Now, I'm not going to simply rely on *Proverbs 8*. I want you to see what it would say about Christ if we did that. Let's read a couple of verses and I'll show you what I'm talking about.

Pro 8:22 The LORD possessed me in the beginning of his way, before his works of old.

Pro 8:23 I was set up from everlasting [That word "set up" means "anointed." He was poured upon, he was anointed], *from the beginning, or ever the earth was.* [*I was set up* (anointed) *from everlasting, from the beginning, or ever the earth was.*]

Pro 8:24 When there were no depths, I was brought forth; [and "brought forth" is "born"] *when there were no fountains abounding with water.*

Pro 8:25 Before the mountains were settled, before the hills was I brought forth: [or I was born]

You can see that if Christ is the wisdom of God and we came over to *Proverbs 8* and said, well he is speaking of Christ here, **THAT CREATES HAVOC IN PEOPLE'S MINDS, TO THINK THAT CHRIST WAS BORN IN ETERNITY.** I know of at least one denomination that uses *Proverbs 8* to **try** to say Christ was created. Yet, he **wasn't** created, we know that. **But was he BORN?** There's a big difference between being created and being born. This verse is using the word "brought forth" (Strong's #2342 in Hebrew). Can I do that? Does the Bible support the concepts that are brought forth in *Proverbs 8*? Does it support that about Christ? Let's look at that verse again:

Pro 8:22 The LORD possessed me in the beginning of his way, **before his** [God's] **works of old.**

What **are** God's "works of old"? Is he talking about creation? Could I say, (if this were talking about Christ) that he would say "the Lord possessed me in the beginning of his way before creation"? See, "before his works of old" because **we know Christ was the Creator.** How would all that fit into this? Does it even fit into this?

Rev 3:14 And unto the angel [messenger] *of the church of the Laodiceans write; These things saith the Amen, the faithful and true witness,* **the beginning of the creation of God;**

So, here is a verse that, if I were to look at *Proverbs 8*, I could say it's talking about wisdom, but it's **a picture of Christ**. He's **personified** Jesus Christ. Christ himself says in *Revelation 3: 14 — I'm the beginning of the creation of God.* That connects with *Ephesians 3: 9 - God created*

all things through Jesus Christ, and I think in our past two studies, we're beginning to see there is **God the Father**, and **there is the Son of God (the God of Israel). Through the Son of God** (if we take all the scriptures and put them together) we see that the **Father created all things through Jesus Christ!** So, it would only make sense what Christ said in *Revelation 3 - I am the BEGINNING of the creation of God*. **Not that he was created, but he was the BEGINNING OF GOD'S CREATION. God had him,** "brought him forth" and "created all things," which is basically what that would mean to me.

Look again at *Proverbs 8:*

Pro 8:22 The LORD possessed me in the beginning of his way, before his works of old. [You could note *Revelation 3: 14* in your Bible.]

Pro 8:23 I was set up [h5258 anointed] *from everlasting, from the beginning, or ever the earth was.*

This word *"anointing,"* to *"be anointed"* – the Old Testament word for **"anointed"** is **"Messiah."** He became **Messiah, the Anointed One.** The New Testament word for that is "Christ." "Christ" is Greek - it means **"THE ANOINTED ONE."** "Christ" and "Messiah" are saying the same thing in two different languages. If you throw in the third language (English) you would have **"anointed one"** – **Messiah/ Christ/Anointed One**. What we just read in *Ephesians 3:9 – that God created all things through Jesus Christ*, he refers to him as "the Anointed One" **before creation.** <u>He created all things through Jesus Christ</u>.

Hebrew word – *Messiah*

Greek word – *Christ*

English word – *Anointed One*

Another scripture is *Philippians 2:5-6.*

Php 2:5 Let this mind be in you, which was also in Christ Jesus:

Php 2:6 Who, being in the form of God, thought it not robbery to be equal with God:

That word "robbery" is an interesting word. It's Old English, and it means **something to be taken, something to be snatched.** He thought it was not something to be taken to be equal with God. He was not seeking equality with God. So many people have used that to say he was equal with God - that's saying he chose **NOT** to be - **HE DIDN'T WANT TO BE EQUAL WITH GOD.** The point I'm making here is:

Php 2:5 Let this mind be in you, which was also in Christ Jesus:

Php 2:6 Who, being in the form of God, thought it not robbery to be equal with God:

See what he's doing? He puts "Jesus, the Anointed One" in time past, in eternity past. God created all things through Jesus Christ. **Before creation, he was the Christ,** so hence, when we look at this in *Proverbs 8* that "I was anointed" – see, "**from the beginning I was anointed in the past, I was anointed in eternity.**" That fits exactly with the way Paul is using "Jesus the Christ."

Pro 8:24 When there were no depths, I was brought forth; when there were no fountains abounding with water.

Pro 8:25 Before the mountains were settled, before the hills was I brought forth:

It looks like **before creation** (and according to this), **WISDOM WAS BORN.** But **WISDOM PERSONIFIED, is that CHRIST?** Is there anything in the Bible speaking of him being born in eternity?

Mic 5:2 But thou, Bethlehem Ephratah,…[Bethlehem is the literal city where Christ was born] …

Mic 5:2 But thou, Bethlehem Ephratah, though thou be little among the thousands of Judah, yet out of thee [yet out of you, Bethlehem] *shall he come forth unto me that is to be ruler in Israel* [this is a prophecy about the birth of Jesus Christ]; *whose goings forth* [h4163 origin] *have been from of old, from everlasting* [or from eternity].

The word "goings forth" [h4163] in Hebrew literally is the word origin. **His origin is from old, from everlasting**.

Have you ever considered Jesus Christ as Creator, as the God of Israel, having an **Origin – originating from**? This fits exactly with what he is saying in *Proverbs 8*. **He was brought forth BEFORE anything was created.** He was **brought forth - he ORIGINATED in eternity!** Why is that so hard for people to accept? This **DOES NOT DENY THE TRINITY**. There is **a Father, there is a Son, and there is a Holy Spirit. What that denies is THEIR DEFINITION of the Trinity.** There's nothing wrong with trinitarian concepts in the Bible. The problem is that they have taken it and made something of it that should not be. What they are saying concerning the Trinity is not true; in **the Trinity, itself, we see a Father, a Son, and Holy Spirit.**

Mat 28:18 And Jesus came and spoke unto them, saying, All power is given unto me in heaven and in earth. [Which shows it was given to him; the Father and Son ARE NOT EQUAL. All power was GIVEN TO him.]

Mat 28:19 Go ye therefore, and teach all nations, baptizing them in the name of the Father, and of the Son, and of the Holy Ghost: [That word "ghost" is Spirit.]

When we talk about baptizing, I know we think of getting in the water, getting dunked in the water and raised back up and you're baptized. But, you see, you wouldn't get in the water unless you were told something and the "telling," giving you the water of the word, immerses you in that truth. So, when he says "go into all nations," he doesn't necessarily mean "make sure you get them all dunked under water" – he is saying "teach them of the Father, Son and Holy Spirit." Today these churches will use this verse and they'll say, "See, there's the Trinity." Well, okay, I see the Father, Son and Holy Spirit, **but where does that give you the right to say they're co-equal and co-eternal?** The Bible does not bear that out. <u>The Bible simply does not say what they are saying it does</u> and just because they find a verse with Father, Son, and Holy Spirit in it - that's supposed to mean they're co-eternal, co-equal? That's fabricated. **THAT IS NOT THE TRUTH**.

We have read in the first two studies, and now in this one, verses that TOTALLY contradict what we have been taught about the Trinity.

Like I've said, I wanted to do a STAR Project to make this simple. I didn't say it's going to be easy to swallow - I said let's make it simple. **If you choose to go along with your organized religion versus the scripture, then you're doing that to yourself - you're condemning yourself - because this is how the love of God is manifest to us.**

Rom 8:32 He that spared not his own Son, but delivered him up for us all, how shall he not with him also freely give us all things?

If anything disproves the church's definition of the Trinity, that does. *He that spared not his own son but delivered him up for us all, how shall he not WITH HIM freely give us all things?* When you throw in there the lie that the Father and Son are co-eternal, then God gave us nothing. According to the scripture, God so loved the world he gave you **his only begotten Son. Was he the only begotten Son?**

Personify *Proverbs 8* and you'll see Jesus Christ born in eternity past. You'll see Jesus Christ, anointed in eternity past. The beauty of that is that the rest of the Bible bears that out. You don't need *Proverbs 8* to see that. All we really need to do is come before God in solitude. Pray and ask him.

LET HIM INSPIRE YOUR HEART.

LET HIM INSPIRE YOUR THINKING.

1Jn 4:9 In this was manifested the love of God toward us, because that God sent his only begotten Son into the world, that we might live through him.

Two things about this...

#1: This shows you how much God loves you. If Jesus was REALLY his Son, then God REALLY loves you like you would a child, **because that was his Son! That was the price he was willing to pay to REDEEM you from iniquity, to get you to THINK differently – to SEE differently.** If you try to tell me that they're co-equal and co-eternal, then that verse doesn't have any love in it.

One pastor tried to tell me that they were **role-playing** – that it really wasn't the son – they were just role-playing. THEY ARE NOT ROLE-PLAYING. **Jesus Christ IS the Son of God and he WAS the Son of God from eternity past.**

#2: God brought forth his Son to help us. Remember *Revelation 13: 8? Christ is the Lamb slain from the foundation of the world,* meaning he was born to give his life to help us. He was *brought forth* by God, *anointed* by God, to help us. Remember what Jesus said to Pilate? *"For this reason was I born and for this cause came I into the world, that I might bear witness to the truth." (John 18:37)* Two births in that verse: For this reason **was I born** and for this cause **came I into the world.** Jesus came into the world through Bethlehem as a babe in a manger. He was the God of Israel. He was born to bear witness to the truth. **That's exactly what he did.** Now, can we accept the truth and follow the Lamb wheresoever he goes, or are we going to try to cling to a denominational group that has no life in and of itself? The life comes from Jesus Christ. **HE SAYS he's the only begotten Son of God.**

I believe it. I've always believed it, but I was told so many things that it was hard to work my way through it. Hence, now I'm sitting here trying to help you. It really is very simple – just take it to the Lord and He will convince you in your own heart that Jesus is his Son.

TRINITY PART D
HOLY SPIRIT

And on the 6ᵗʰ day... God said,
Let us make man in our image...
This day this scripture is being fulfilled in our ears.

Hi. I'm Scott Stanley, founder of DTG Ministries and this is the fourth part of our STAR Project on the Trinity. Today we're going to be talking about the Holy Spirit. I know the Holy Spirit is a vast subject discussing all the scriptures available to us. Let's begin by comparing two verses to help us understand **WHAT the Holy Spirit is**. The first verse is found in *Isaiah:*

Isa 40:13 Who hath directed the <u>Spirit</u> of the LORD, or being his counsellor hath taught him?

Let's compare that with *1Corinthians 2:16.*

1Co 2:16 For who hath known the <u>mind</u> of the Lord, that he may instruct him? But we have the mind of Christ.

In *1Corinthians 2:16* Paul is quoting *Isaiah 40*. Look at the words he uses for **Spirit**. Paul uses the word **"mind."** This is why I began to realize "mind and spirit" are synonymous throughout the Bible. Let's examine more verses: *Proverbs 29:11.*

Pro 29:11 A fool utters all his mind [h7307-spirit]: *but a wise man keeps it in till afterwards.*

The word "MIND" is **LITERALLY** the word "SPIRIT." I think when King James translated this it didn't make sense to them to say you "utter your spirit," so they put the word "mind." **But it literally is "spirit."** *Gen 26:35 Which were a grief of mind* [h7303-spirit] *unto Isaac and to Rebekah.* Again, we read about grief of "spirit." Another verse is *Proverbs 1:23.*

*Pro 1:23 Turn you at my reproof: behold, I will pour out my spirit unto you, I will make known **my words** unto you.*

Proverbs 1:23 - I will pour out my spirit. There are prophecies where God is going to pour out his Spirit or pour out of his Spirit. Here is a Bible definition of what that means: *"I'll pour out my spirit – I will make known my words unto you."* Here is another verse:

Eze 2:1 And he said unto me, Son of man, stand upon thy feet, and I will speak unto thee.

Eze 2:2 And the spirit entered into me when he spoke unto me, and set me upon my feet, that I heard him that spoke unto me.

What I want you to see is that the **"spirit" and "mind" are SYNONYMOUS**. How do we convey our spirit? How do you share your spirit? With words. Really, the "spirit" is another way of saying your understanding. It could be **the truth that you possess**. It's just how you see something. **Your "spirit" - YOU CONVEY IT WITH WORDS.**

Let's look at *1Corinthians 2:10.*

1Co 2:10 But God hath revealed them [these things] *unto us by his Spirit* [by his understanding, by his truth]: *for the Spirit searches* [the truth searches] *all things, yea, the deep things of God.*

1Co 2:11 For what man knows the things of a man, save [except] *the spirit of man* [the understanding of the man] *which is in him? even so the things of God knows no man, but the Spirit of God* [You could say which is in him].

1Co 2:12 Now we have received, not the spirit of the world [the understanding of the world], *but the spirit* [the understanding] *which is of God; that we might know the things that are freely given to us of God.*

One thing that is clear to us all: The world has its own understanding - it has its truth, **but God has his truth**. God's truth consists of him, his son, salvation, humanity, and creation. The truth of God is old. It's high. **The TRUTH of God is HIS SPIRIT.** The world has its truth. God has his truth. **God's truth is SEPARATE from the world's truth.** To be separated is the word "holy." Hence, you have the world's truth, the world's understanding - the spirit of the world, and you have God's holy truth, God's holy understanding – Holy Spirit. When you receive his Spirit, you are IN the world, but you're not OF the world anymore. You're carrying TRUTH that goes all the way back to eternity past. **In your earthen vessel, you're carrying ETERNAL TRUTH.**

We just saw how the Spirit is conveyed using words. Let's build on that with *John 3:33.*

John 3:33 He that hath received his [Christ's] *testimony hath set to his seal that God is true.*

If you believe in Christ, you believe in God. Why?

John 3:34 For he whom God hath sent speaks the words of God: for God giveth not the Spirit by measure unto him.

"Spirit and words." The Father gave his Son his spirit without measure. He gave him his understanding. He gave him **Holy Truth** (Holy Spirit) and Christ is speaking the words that God gave him. Yet another step:

John 6:63 It is the spirit that quickens; the flesh profits nothing: the words that I speak unto you, they are spirit, and they are life.

From the Father to the Son, the spirit and words… from Christ to us, "the words" he says, "I speak, are spirit." But what about between each other? From the Father to the Son, to the Son to us. But what about right now? What's happening right now between us?

John 7:38 He that believeth on me, as the scripture hath said, out of his belly shall flow rivers of living water.

John 7:39 (But this spoke he of the Spirit, which they that believe on him should receive: For the Holy Ghost [Spirit] *was not yet given; because that Jesus was not yet glorified.)*

Two things about this verse:

1: Out of your belly will flow rivers of living water. This spoke he of the Spirit. **Your belly**, literal belly (where you eat bread and it goes into your belly**) is a symbol of your mind. If you eat the bread of Christ, that goes into your belly** (pointing to the head). So, *out of your belly will flow rivers of living water. This spoke he of the Spirit.* **The Spirit comes through your mouth in the words you speak**.

2: What does he mean, "the Spirit was not yet given because Jesus was not yet glorified"? Because what happened at that cross is pregnant with truth. When Jesus died on that cross, he died to redeem us from iniquity. The way that takes place on the cross (through what he portrays there and what he shows us) had not yet happened. Jesus would be crucified on that cross, be made sin, die, and be raised from the dead. Until that happened, the truths that contain that Spirit (the truth of that Spirit) were not yet given because it hadn't happened yet. **Jesus was going to LIVE and PORTRAY that so that WE could understand more elements of God's Truth.** Let's take another step.

John 14:15 If ye love me, keep my commandments.

John 14:16 And I will pray the Father, and he shall give you another Comforter, that he may abide with you for ever;

John 14:17 Even the Spirit of truth; whom the world cannot receive, because it sees him not, neither knows him: but ye know him [you know this Comforter]; *for he dwelleth with you* [present tense, he dwells with you now], *and shall be in you* [future].

John 14:18 I will not leave you comfortless [orphans]: *I will come to you.*

It's interesting that **Christ refers to himself as the Comforter.** "**I** will come to you; **I'm** not going to leave you orphans - I'm going to come to you. I'm going to send you **ANOTHER Comforter**." Why another? Because like we saw in *John 7*, **what happened at the cross and the resurrection had not happened yet.** When all of that takes place, then he becomes **ANOTHER COMFORTER. He will have truth to give you that he didn't have UNTIL he was glorified.**

1Jn 2:1 My little children, these things write I unto you, that ye sin not. And if any man sin, we have an advocate [g3875 comforter] *with the Father, Jesus Christ the righteous:*

Guess what? The word "advocate" is Comforter. **That is the same word used in *John 14*.** What comes to your mind when you see "**advocate**" versus "**comforter**"? There you see that old concept "Jesus has to protect us from God." When you say "advocate," that brings to mind a lawyer or somebody who's advocating for you. Whereas, when you make it the "comforter," that's another story. Why would Christ refer to himself as a "comforter"? Why would John say, "he's the comforter - if you sin, don't worry, you've got a comforter"? Because this is seen in something we've read already.

1Co 1:30 But of him [or of God] *are ye in Christ Jesus, who of God is made unto us wisdom, and righteousness, and sanctification, and redemption:*

What does that mean? **If you want to understand God and his salvation, then you go to the cross, and you see the death of his Son. And "in" Jesus Christ, we see God's wisdom. We see God's righteousness. We see our redemption and our sanctification.** It's all wrapped up in the only begotten son of God. JESUS IS that element of truth of God. Do you want to talk about God's redemption? Try doing it without mentioning the cross! What about God's salvation? God's righteousness? God's wisdom? Do that without mentioning the cross. **CHRIST IS THAT SPIRIT.**

2Co 3:17 Now the Lord is that Spirit: and where the Spirit of the Lord is, there is liberty.

Now Christ encompasses all of that: Salvation, redemption, righteousness, the wisdom of God. **CHRIST IS THAT TRUTH** God has given us. Think about it - it's all wrapped up in the only begotten Son of God. **Now the Lord is that Spirit because he has lived it.** Now that Spirit can be given because he has been glorified. When he gave that spirit in *Acts 2*, where did that come from?

Act 2:32 This Jesus hath [**the**] *God raised up* [that word 'God' has the definite article in front of it. It literally is THE God or THE Divine One], ...

Act 2:32 This Jesus hath [**the**] *God* [Divine One] *raised up, whereof we all are witnesses.*

Act 2:33 Therefore being by the right hand of [**the**] *God* [Divine One] *exalted, and having received of the Father the promise of the Holy Ghost* [Spirit], *he* [Jesus] *hath shed forth this, which ye now see and hear.*

Where did the Spirit come from? It came from the Father. We've already seen that in *John 3* where the Father gave him his Spirit without measure. **Jesus Christ was given the PROMISE of a Holy Understanding, a deeper understanding, which he received when he lived his life as a man**.

It's one thing to tell somebody something, and another to experience it. If I told you how to drive a car, you could read the book and think of what I said. That's NOT the same thing as what will happen when you get in the car, turn that key, put it in reverse and try to back out of the driveway. Suddenly the reality of what you're doing will hit you. You will learn volumes more by driving the car than by reading the book. By reading the book, you'll find rules and regulations. Behind the steering wheel, you'll learn how to drive a car.

Well, **when the Son of God became a man, the things that he experienced deepened his understanding of God, of himself, and of humanity**. Christ BECAME the VERY ESSENCE OF GOD'S LOVE. And sacrifice. And sanctification. And righteousness for you.

HE BECAME THAT WHOLE ASPECT OF GOD'S SPIRIT.

Col 2:9 For in him [or in Christ] *dwelleth all the fulness of the Godhead bodily.*

Col 2:10 And ye are complete in him, which is the head of all principality and power:

Now here is a word introduced to us, "**Godhead**." Personally, I have begun to use "Godhead" to replace "Trinity." The "Trinity," again, if you see the Father, Son, and Holy Spirit - and you want to say that's a "trinity" - well, there is an element of truth to that. But, again, the way the universal church defines it, makes it untrue. If you stick with a Bible word, in this case, "Godhead," that word seems to include all of it. If you say **"Godhead,"** that **implies a Head God, which is the Father.** *To us there's only one God, the Father. (1Cor 8:6)* **The Holy Spirit is the Truth of God.** *(1John 5:6).* That is why we see this in *1John 5: 7.*

1Jn 5:7 For there are three that bear record in heaven, the Father, the Word, and the Holy Ghost [Spirit]: *and **these three are one**.*

THIS is a verse people would use to try to prove that the Trinity exists - they are co-equal, co-eternal. **Yet NOTHING in that verse says that.** It says, *"THE FATHER, THE WORD, AND THE HOLY GHOST (SPIRIT) ARE ONE."* What does it mean to be "ONE"?

*John 17:22 And the glory which thou gave me I have given them; **that they may be one, even as we are one**:*

What does it mean to be one with God? Does that mean that you are a part of the Godhead? No. **To be one with God means you're in unity with God. THE FATHER, THE SON, AND THE HOLY SPIRIT ARE ALL ONE.** They're all in perfect unity. *The Church has been baptized by the Spirit INTO the body of Christ. (1Corinthians 12:13)* That makes us one with them. The thing that makes us one is the Spirit of God. God's Spirit is that glue that binds the Father and Son AND humanity.

We all are one in Jesus Christ, and **the ULTIMATE TRINITY is the FATHER, the SON and HUMANITY, BOUND TOGETHER by the HOLY SPIRIT.** Glued together, we're all one in Christ.

THE LAW PART A
ROMANS 7

Hi, I'm Scott Stanley. This is DTG Ministries giving you another STAR Project - this one is on the law. In the first segment of this STAR Project, we will look at the law. The first thing I want to point out is who actually gave the law. Who gave the law at Sinai?

Let's turn in our Bibles to *Hebrews*. I want to start reading Chapter 9, verse 15:

Heb 9:15 And for this cause he is the mediator of the new testament, that by means of death, for the redemption of the transgressions that were under the first testament, they which are called might receive the promise of eternal inheritance.

Heb 9:16 For where a testament is, there must also of necessity be the death of the testator.

Obviously, **Christ is the one who gave the testament** or gave the covenant because **it required the death of the one who gave it** or the testator. Let's keep investigating this and let's turn back to *Jeremiah 31.*

Jer 31:31 Behold, the days come, saith the LORD, that I will make a new covenant with the house of Israel, and with the house of Judah:

Jer 31:32 Not according to the covenant that I made with their fathers in the day that I took them by the hand to bring [to lead] *them out of the land of Egypt; which my covenant they brake, although I was an husband unto them, saith the LORD:*

Two things: 1) **The one who gave the covenant at Sinai is the same one who gave the new covenant.** (*I'm going to make a new covenant; not like the one I made before.*) I'm going to make a new covenant with you and there must be the death of the one who makes that covenant. 2) The second thing about what we're reading here in *Jeremiah 31*, is that **he refers to himself as a husband unto them**. He was a husband unto the Jews. Now let's look at one more verse, *Psalm 68:8*.

Psalms 68:8 The earth shook, the heavens also dropped at the presence of God: even Sinai itself was moved at the presence of God, <u>the God of Israel</u>.

So, here is another name to give Jesus: **He is the God of Israel - the God of Israel who came down on Sinai.** It was the God of Israel that **gave both covenants**. It was the God of Israel **who had to give his life**, and it was the God of Israel **who referred to HIMSELF as a husband unto them**. All of these things are highly significant in understanding the law. In fact, it's crucial that you understand what was going on at Sinai – WHO THAT WAS and the fact he was going to have to give his life for the second covenant. **The same guy that gave the first covenant gave the second. He had to give his life and he was a husband unto the Jew.** Let's turn to *Romans, Chapter 7*. I want to start reading at verse 1, and I just ask you to receive the truth with an open heart.

Rom 7:1 Know ye not, brethren, (for I speak to them that know the law,) how that the law hath dominion over a man as long as he lives?

Rom 7:2 For the woman which hath an husband is bound by the law to her husband so long as he lives; but if the husband be dead, she is loosed from the law of her husband.

Rom 7:3 So then if, while her husband lives, she be married to another man, she shall be called an adulteress: but if her husband be dead, she is free from that law; so that she is no adulteress, though she be married to another man.

Rom 7:4 Wherefore, my brethren, ye also are become dead to the law by the body of Christ; that ye should be married to another, even to him who is raised from the dead, that we should bring forth fruit unto God.

What did we just read here? There is an understanding found in the law that when a man and woman are married, if the husband dies, she is free from that man. Christ said, "I'm a husband to you." **He died fulfilling that concept, that law.** Let's look at it like this:

Let's say I make a list of things that I want my wife to do every day, or get specific things done once a week. You know, whatever it is - I want the laundry done. I want the house cleaned; I want food on the table. I want her to go shopping. I want her to do this and this and this, and then the day comes that I die. Is she still held accountable for doing all of those things I wanted her to do? No. When the husband is dead, the wife is free from that law. **Christ was the husband**.

Remember, in *Matthew 5:17*, he said, *I have come to fulfill the law. I'm not going to destroy it; I've come to fulfill it*. Well, I was always told he fulfilled it by living it, in keeping the law. **No, he was the husband - he FULFILLED it by giving his life**. By means of the death of Christ, according to what Paul just told us, **we are free from the law by the body of Christ**. He says, I'm telling you guys who know the law (who understand the law - the husband and the wife) when the husband is dead, the wife is free. Christ said, *"I'm your husband."* Christ said, *"I've come to fulfill the law."* So, what replaces the law? What is it that takes the place of the law?

I am NOT saying that you just live lawless. I'm NOT saying that you do anything you want because there are no Ten Commandments anymore. No, that isn't what this means. **It DOES mean you're FREE FROM THE LAW BY THE BODY OF CHRIST, but now YOU ARE FREE TO WALK IN LOVE**. Remember *Romans 13*.

Rom 13:8 Owe no man any thing, but to love one another: for he that loveth another hath fulfilled the law.

Rom 13:10 Love worketh no ill to his neighbor: therefore love is the fulfilling of the law.

Owe no man anything, but to love one another, FOR LOVE is the FULFILLMENT OF THE LAW. He never says the law fulfills love. **LOVE FULFILLS THE LAW**.

The God of Israel came down on Sinai!
The God of Israel gave the covenants!
The God of Israel was the testator who gave his life!
The God of Israel is Jesus Christ!

THE LAW PART B
THE LAW IS SPIRITUAL

This is the second installment of a STAR Project on the law. We saw in Part A that we are free from the law by the body of Christ and that love fulfills the law. What I want to do is get into that, just a little bit more.

The Apostle Paul wrote in *Romans 13 (Romans 13:8, 10)* that love is a fulfillment of the law. I want to explain how that is. The first verse that I want you to look at is in *Romans, Chapter 7.*

Rom 7:14 For we know that the law is spiritual: but I am carnal, sold under sin.

"The law is spiritual." What does he mean by the law is spiritual? Throughout the Bible, spirit and mind are synonymous so when something is spiritual, it's of the mind. That would just be another way of saying it - it's of the mind. What do you mean, of the mind? I want to give you a couple of examples that Jesus gave us in *Matthew, Chapter 5.*

Mat 5:21 Ye have heard that it was said by them of old time, Thou shalt not kill; and whosoever shall kill shall be in danger of the judgment:

Mat 5:22 But I say unto you, That whosoever is angry with his brother without a cause shall be in danger of the judgment: and whosoever shall say to his brother, Raca, shall be in danger of the council: but whosoever shall say, Thou fool, shall be in danger of hell fire.

That word "**hell**" is "Gehenna." Strong's number [1067] - *James 3:5-6* refers to hell as anger. The tongue is a fire, set on fire of hell [1067]. Another one is in verse 27.

Mat 5:27 Ye have heard that it was said by them of old time, Thou shalt not commit adultery:

Mat 5:28 But I say unto you, That whosoever looks on a woman to lust after her hath committed adultery with her already in his heart.

What are we seeing here? We're seeing **this outward action of murder. Jesus says that means don't get angry. He just took this physical, literal murder and put it within the mind**. If you don't even get angry, you'll never commit murder! The same with adultery. You've been told not to commit adultery. I tell you don't even lust in your heart. **Jesus took that outward action and put it within the human heart**.

Again, Paul says *the law is spiritual*, and I have learned to recognize that **we can take all of this law and put it inward**. Now, if I am angry or if I am considering murder, or considering adultery and he says don't even get angry, how do you do that? How do you prevent the anger from happening? Remember: <u>Thoughts produce feelings, and feelings move you to action</u>. So, if you can change that thought that makes you feel angry, you will not follow through and commit murder. If you can change that thought that's causing you to lust, you will not follow through with adultery.

Jesus Christ died to redeem us from all iniquity. **The thought** that leads to anger, to murder, **that thought is iniquity**. **The thought** that leads you to lust and commit adultery, **that thought is iniquity**. The question is, **how does Christ's death redeem me from iniquity**? Because by changing that thought, I would act in love toward my enemy! By changing that thought, (instead of committing adultery) I would be able to act in love toward that person, toward my wife.

It is the thought that needs to be changed, and it is an awareness of love - walking in love that will prevent you from sin. When we see Christ on the cross, we're aware of the fact that Paul said: *He that knew no sin was made to be sin, so that we might be made the righteousness of God*. How was Jesus made sin? Remember, the man didn't sin. HE NEVER SINNED. How was he made to be a sin? How do you take somebody who hasn't sinned and say they're made to be sin?

Jesus portrayed on that cross the outward picture of the inward truth of all humanity.

Crown of thorns: Christ's crown of thorns was a symbol of our guilt - those things that prick your mind. You think about it later and it bothers you - you can't hardly go there thinking about what you've done.

Stripes: The stripes on Jesus' back were a symbol of things that have been told to us - ways that we have been hurt, that we're just not able to let it go; we're not able to forgive. The stripes on Jesus' back were not what we deserve - it's what has already happened to all of us - the pain caused by other people.

Nakedness: Nakedness is when you expose yourself with your own anger, your own lust, and your own ideas.

Darkness of the land: The darkness that happened - the land was dark; the sun was blotted out. It is a symbol of our lack of understanding of God. **God is light.** *(1John 1:5)* When you're in darkness, you don't know God and that is what you're seeing Christ portray on the cross.

Christ had no guilt but he's wearing a crown of thorns. **He forgave everybody**. Remember, *"Father, forgive them for they know not what they do,"* yet the stripes on his back were a symbol of our unwillingness to do that. His nakedness, and the darkness, **all portrayed humanity without a knowledge of God.**

So, if we're standing at that cross, we see ourselves. We see what we have done to others - the crown of thorns, the guilt, and what others have done to us - the stripes on the back, and we realize that God completely understands us. Just like Christ said, *"Father, forgive them for they know not what they do"* - we can receive that truth. We can receive that, too. When we did what we did, we didn't know what we were doing; we didn't understand it. That's no different than the soldiers who were killing Jesus; they were all forgiven by Christ. If he can forgive them, he can forgive us; and if he has forgiven us, **he has forgiven all of us**.

So, the anger I'm carrying toward people who have hurt me, I can let that go and love them! Once I realize that I am forgiven, that we are forgiven, then I can realize that those problems that you have had in your life from the guilt and the stripes - I don't need to cause any more of it. See, I can look at the cross and I can see God forgiving me. I can see God forgiving you, and I can also see the things I have caused - when I've said what I've said to you, when I've done what I've done to you - and I can realize I don't want to do that anymore. I don't want to cause any more pain. I don't want to hurt you anymore.

By means of the cross, when he died - the husband died - it set the wife free. But he also gives you a new covenant. That new covenant will allow you to know him and live according to his will. He will give you a new spirit and you can live according to the will of God.

God is love.

Love (God) does not make a record of
sin, and we are free to live in freedom from
iniquity.

Rom 13:8 Owe no man any thing, but to love one another:

for he that loveth another hath fulfilled the law.

THE LAW PART C
THE SIXTH DAY

The Deep Things of God are being explored here. This is the third segment of a STAR Project on the law. I want to cover something that maybe you have never heard before. I want to be able to take my time and make it crystal clear as to what I believe the scriptures are telling us. We're constantly searching for the deep things of God and trying to simplify it.

In the last study, reading *Romans 7:14*, I made the comment that the law is spiritual. We were able to see where Christ brought this out himself in *Matthew 5*, when he said, "*You have been told don't commit murder, I tell you, don't even get angry.*" **He took all of the things that we read and put it within the human heart, making them of the mind or spiritual.** So today, we are going to build on that, but I'm going to come through the back door, so to speak. I want to share with you some things that add up to the law being spiritual. But when you see what is actually written in the scripture compared to what we have been told, it's shocking. I would ask you to bear with me as we go over these things. Let's begin by reading *Genesis, Chapter 1*, starting at verse 26.

Gen 1:26 And God said, Let us make man in our image, after our likeness: and let them have dominion over the fish of the sea, and over the fowl of the air, and over the cattle, and over all the earth, and over every creeping thing that creeps upon the earth.

Gen 1:27 So God created man in his own image, in the image of God created he him; male and female created he them.

What are we reading? This is creation week, and what we're reading happens on the sixth day of creation. It's interesting that he gives man dominion over all things. Let's pick this up in *Psalms 8*, reading from verse 5.

Psa 8:5 For thou hast made him a little lower than the angels, and hast crowned him with glory and honor.

Psa 8:6 Thou made him to have dominion over the works of thy hands; thou hast put all things under his feet:

Psa 8:7 All sheep and oxen, yea, and the beasts of the field;

Psa 8:8 The fowl of the air, and the fish of the sea, and whatsoever passes through the paths of the seas.

I believe the psalmist is repeating the concept we saw in *Genesis 1*, that on the sixth day God makes man in his image (after his likeness) and gives him dominion over all things. Let's turn to *Hebrews, Chapter 2*.

Heb 2:5 For unto the angels hath he not put in subjection the world to come, whereof we speak.

Heb 2:6 But one in a certain place testified, saying, What is man, that thou art mindful of him? or the son of man, that thou visit him? [He is simply quoting *Psalms 8*]

Heb 2:7 Thou made him a little lower than the angels; thou crowned him with glory and honor, and didst set him over the works of thy hands:

Heb 2:8 Thou hast put all things in subjection under his feet. For in that he put all in subjection under him, he left nothing that is not put under him. But now [right now] *we see not yet all things put under him.*

Heb 2:9 But we see Jesus, who was made a little lower than the angels for the suffering of death, crowned with glory and honor; that he by the grace of God should taste death for every man.

Look again at the end of **verse 8**: …**But NOW we see NOT YET all things put under him**. What is he saying? What does this have to do with anything concerning the law being spiritual and what we've been studying? If you paid close attention to what we just read, the writer of *Hebrews*, who I believe to be Paul, quotes *Psalms 8*. *Psalms 8* is a depiction of *Genesis 1*, when on the sixth day, God makes man in his own image. The catch is, when you look at *Hebrews Chapter 2*, **Paul says that hasn't happened yet**.

I know people who have read *Genesis* and believe God made us in His image and put all things under our feet, **but Paul says it hasn't happened yet**! You do not have all things under your feet. He says everything that passes through the sea, you have dominion over it. Well, let's see. If you jump in some water with a shark, tell me how much dominion you have over that thing. You don't have dominion over everything like he said you would have. So, what does this mean? Let's just turn to *Genesis 2*, starting with verse 1.

Gen 2:1 Thus the heavens and the earth were finished, and all the host of them.

Gen 2:2 And on the seventh day God ended his work which he had made; and he rested on the seventh day from all his work which he had made.

Now, who is that host that's been made complete? Is he talking about the literal stars in heaven and they're not finished yet? No. I want to give you a different idea of how to see what you're reading in *Genesis*. What you are reading in *Genesis* is talking about the creation of the church, not the universe. When you look at the seven days of creation, you are looking at the steps a believer goes through to come to the place where he is made complete - like he stated in *Genesis 2*, the host was made complete.

On the sixth day he puts all things under your feet. All INIQUITY is put under your feet, and you, then, are made in the image of God because you understand iniquity and you choose to allow that atoning thought to take the place of your anger, or whatever it is that's happening to you – your lust. What's happening that's making you angry? Well, you replace that thought with righteousness, looking at it the way God does. In so doing, you are made free from that sin, and you are made in the image of God. He puts all things under your feet. What you're reading in *Genesis* is more of a **prophecy**, that when the host is made complete, God can rest.

Remember when Christ said that *my father works hitherto and I work.* *(John 5:17)* **God has NEVER rested since he made man**. He has been working for our salvation to help us. He has never taken that rest. Now, am I making this up? No. Paul states in *Hebrews 2*, he puts all things under our feet but we don't see that yet. **That means the sixth day of creation has not finished and God has not entered into a Sabbath rest**.

This connects with the law because of that fourth commandment - you've got to keep the Sabbath. Why would God do that? What is God trying to help us see that we might understand and have a closer walk with him and his only begotten son? What is it we need to understand? **James makes the statement** (concerning the law) **if you have broken one of the laws of the commandments you've broken them all.** *(James 2:10)* How could that be? I'm telling you, it's because all of the commandments are saying the same thing. The reason I wanted to bring this out about the Sabbath is because it's very easy to see. It's one of the easiest ones to see.

Once you see this principle, you can apply it to all the other commandments and understand what Paul meant in ***Romans 7:14 - The law of God is spiritual.*** **It happens in your own heart, between your own ears**. The law of God is spiritual. The sixth day of creation is not complete. We see not yet all things put under our feet. What happens when everything is put under our feet?

1Co 15:22 For as in Adam all die, even so in Christ shall all be made alive.

1Co 15:23 But every man in his own order: Christ the firstfruits; afterward they that are Christ's at his coming.

1Co 15:24 Then cometh the end, when he shall have delivered up the kingdom to God, even the Father; when he shall have put down all rule and all authority and power.

1Co 15:25 For he must reign, till he hath put all enemies under his feet.

1Co 15:26 The last enemy that shall be destroyed is death.

1Co 15:27 For he hath put all things under his feet. But when he saith [When it says] *all things are put under him, it is manifest that he is excepted, which did put all things under him.* [It's except the one who put all things under him],

1Co 15:28 And when all things shall be subdued unto him, then shall the Son also himself be subject unto him that put all things under him, that God may be all in all.

What are we reading? **The last thing to be put under our feet, the last enemy is death.** When he puts all things under our feet, you will have dominion over all things - you will have life, and he will deliver up the kingdom to his father, who put all things under his feet. Again, in *Genesis 1: 26*, when he says *let us make man in our image after our likeness,* **we are living in that day right now - because it is a spiritual truth. YOU ARE AT THE END OF THE WORLD** and God is putting all things under our feet.

Now, why is it that if I've broken one commandment, I've broken them all? Turn to *Hebrews, Chapter 4.* I'm going to read verses 9 and 10, but really you should spend some time in this whole chapter to understand.

Heb 4:9 There remains therefore a rest to the people of God. [g4520 – That word "rest," is *"a keeping of the Sabbath"* – King James put "rest." *There remains therefore a keeping of the Sabbath to the people of God.*]

Heb 4:10 For he that is entered into his [God's] *rest, he also hath ceased from his own works, as God did from his.*

THERE is the meaning of the Sabbath. The meaning of the Sabbath is to cease from your own works and to do God's works. **And that day, that one day a week that was set aside, was a symbol, a parable of us coming to the place where we only do as the Spirit of God leads us.** That's what the Sabbath meant. You make a choice. Am I going to do what I want to do - do my own works, or am I going to rest in Christ and do as the Spirit leads me?

Look at the very first commandment: YOU SHALL HAVE NO OTHER GODS BEFORE ME. It's saying the same thing. He says, do what I'm telling you - not what your flesh is telling you. **Every commandment is stating that: Do what God wants you to do, not**

what your flesh wants you to do. If you just take the time and read each one of those commandments and think about it - you'll realize **all of them are spiritual**. If I decide I'm going to murder and I let myself get angry, what did I do? **I chose my will over the Spirit of God**.

Every one of them, that's what you must do. So, if you've broken one commandment - if you've chosen your will over God's, then you've broken them all because they all say the same thing. That really is the meaning of the Sabbath. Here we are at the end of the world, trying to come to a deeper understanding of what the scriptures say. I'm not making it up. For now, we see not yet all things put under man.

We're in the sixth day.

God has given us an understanding of what iniquity is.

God has given us an understanding of the meaning of the cross.

God has given us an understanding that Christ died to redeem us from all iniquity and to put all things under our feet.

THE LAW PART D
GOVERNED BY GRACE

The three previous studies on the law revealed that *we are free from the law by the body of Christ (Romans 7:4)* because *Christ was the one who gave the law. Christ was the husband. The husband died, setting the wife free from the law of the husband.* Next, we saw the law was spiritual; *(Romans 7:14)* that Christ applied these meanings of the law to an inward thing: You've been told not to kill; I say don't get angry. The idea of not getting angry - **how does one not get angry? You have to walk in love! LOVE IS THE FULFILLING OF THE LAW.** Then we saw how all of the Ten Commandments are basically stating the same thing *(James 2:10)*; to **put the will of God above your will**.

Now, let's delve into this final section of study with the goal of understanding the God of love that we have. Let's seek out what is to be governing us in this life if we're going to believe in God, believe in Jesus, and trust him for our salvation.

How are we to be governed in life? Let me ask you a simple question. **What does it mean to be "under the law"?** The reason I ask you this is because the history I've had with the universal church has given me a definition of "*under the law*." Many people I've dealt with *wanted* to be "*under the law.*" These individuals thought you should be keeping that law, so when the Bible says you're NOT under the law, these individuals claim that you're not condemned by the law – (in other words) to be under the law means to be condemned by the law. Well, I would like to challenge that. Please turn to *Galatians, Chapter 4*; we'll read verses 19-21.

Gal 4:19 My little children, of whom I travail in birth again until Christ be formed in you,

Gal 4:20 I desire to be present with you now, and to change my voice; for I stand in doubt of you.

Gal 4:21 Tell me, ye that <u>desire to be under the law</u>, do ye not hear the law?

So, if being under the law means you're condemned by the law, then what you just read doesn't make any sense. *"You people who desire to be under the law"* - no one desires to be condemned by it. It means something different: **To be under the law means to be governed by it!**

That is what is being said. *You who desire to be governed by it, do you not hear what it's saying?* So I said the scriptures tell us that YOU'RE NOT UNDER THE LAW. Really, it means that **you're not to be governed by the law.** Let's read this in *Romans 6.*

Rom 6:14 For sin shall not have dominion over you: for ye are not under the law, but under grace.

You are not governed by the law; you're governed by grace. What does Paul mean, "You're governed by grace"? When he says you're governed by grace, he doesn't mean the grace that God is showing you. He means the **grace that you are showing toward others BECAUSE of the grace God has given you**. You're to be governed by grace. And notice how Paul began that verse: ***Sin shall not have dominion over you; YOU'RE TO BE GOVERNED BY GRACE.***

What does that mean? All of my Christian life, I was told that I cannot stop sinning: God's going to have to give me a new body and then I can quit sinning. **Why would anybody say that? It's because they can't quit sinning!** They don't understand it. What is it they don't understand? The power of the Gospel is seen in the cross. Paul stated this about Jesus: *"He gave himself to redeem us from all iniquity."* *(Titus 2:14)*

INIQUITY IS THE THOUGHT YOU HAVE BEFORE YOU SIN. When you have authority in your life over iniquity, YOU WILL NOT SIN. For you to have authority in your life over iniquity, you're going to have to love people. Somebody can make you angry, but you're not governed by the law; you're governed by grace toward that person! **GRACE is to govern you.** You stop, and you consider what is going on: What is making me angry? What is making me lust? What is it that's happening to me? You consider what is happening, and **YOU REPLACE THAT THOUGHT OF ANGER WITH ANOTHER THOUGHT.**

This is what Christ showed us at the cross. *Christ has shown us the soul of humanity: The crown of thorns, the guilt, the stripes - those things you can't forgive or let go of; the nakedness where you expose yourself in your actions, and darkness - the fact that you don't know God; in fact, you don't understand him.* God painted that picture using his son to do it. Christ became sin; he who knew no sin became sin so that we could be made the righteousness of God. **Righteousness is God's understanding,** so when I have a thing going on in my life, God would have me show love toward that person. Another way to put it would be **governed by grace**. Let grace govern your life. What does he mean, "by grace"? *Luke, Chapter 6* is one of my favorite chapters in discussing grace. Let's start with verse 32:

*Luk 6:32 For if ye love them which love you, what **thank** have ye? for sinners also love those that love them.*

The word "thank" is *grace*. Now, look at it again.

*Luk 6:32 For if ye love them which love you, what **thank** [grace] have ye? for sinners also love those that love them.*

*Luk 6:33 And if ye do good to them which do good to you, what **thank** [grace] have ye? for sinners also do even the same.*

*Luk 6:34 And if ye lend to them of whom ye hope to receive, what **thank** [grace] have ye? for sinners also lend to sinners, to receive as much again.*

Luk 6:35 But love ye your enemies, and do good, and lend, hoping for nothing again; and your reward shall be great, and ye shall be the children of the Highest: for he is kind unto the unthankful and to the evil.

Luk 6:36 Be ye therefore merciful, as your Father also is merciful.

Consider what we're reading. ***Sin shall not have dominion over you. You're NOT GOVERNED BY THE LAW – you're to be GOVERNED BY GRACE.*** You take the time to 'atone that thought of iniquity' - replace that thought of iniquity with another thought - something about that person that will cause you to slow down and **have mercy on them.** Let me show you something in *Psalms 78.*

Psa 78:36 Nevertheless they did flatter him with their mouth, and they lied unto him with their tongues.

Psa 78:37 For their heart was not right with him, neither were they stedfast in his covenant.

Psa 78:38 But he, being full of compassion, forgave [or atoned] *their iniquity* [that word "forgave" is the word *atonement*], …

Psa 78:38 But he, being full of compassion, forgave [atoned] *their iniquity, and destroyed them not* [he didn't destroy them]: *yea, many a time turned he his anger away, and did not stir up all his wrath.*

Psa 78:39 For [Because] *he remembered that they were but flesh; a wind that passes away and cometh not again.*

Verse 39, ***"He remembered they were but flesh,"*** **is the ATONEMENT of the INIQUITY.** Instead of being angry with them and destroying them, he remembered they were but flesh. There you see the concept that brings in the cross where Christ is portraying broken humanity.

So, when you start to get angry (or whatever's happening), you can **atone** their iniquity. You can replace that thought with, *"Father, forgive them - they don't know what they're doing."* I remember they are but flesh. I remember they don't really have a connection with God. I have that connection, and I'm more responsible than they are. Whatever that thought is that will cause you to have a different feeling so that you don't act in anger and wrath - that's the atonement - **that's the purpose of the cross: to redeem us from all iniquity.**

That is how you live your life governed by grace. You slow down. You don't add iniquity-to-iniquity, sin-to-sin. **You let the Lord give you another way of seeing humanity.** When you do that, **SIN WILL NOT HAVE DOMINION OVER YOU**.

**You are not governed by the law;
you are governed by grace.**

<u>NOTES</u>

<u>NOTES</u>

<u>NOTES</u>

Printed in the USA
CPSIA information can be obtained
at www.ICGtesting.com
LVHW052013100124
768637LV00027B/1578